The Total

Get Out of Debt

Make-Over

The Combination of Ancient Wisdom
and Modern Technology that Provides
Keys to Financial Freedom

Dan Cavalli

How Debt Ruins Your Life

People who appear to have everything: nice cars, a big house, lots of toys, beautiful clothes, and expensive vacations…are often the most miserable and stressed out people you will ever meet. Why? Much of what they have has been purchased on credit.

They have to continue to make all of their debt payments each month or they will lose their ideal lifestyle. Sometimes, the pressure is just too much. You probably don't own a yacht or have a vacation home overseas. Most people don't.

But that doesn't mean that your level of financial debt isn't ruining your life. In drastic circumstances, financial problems can even result in an early death. Most of the time, however, money problems result in social and financial problems such as marital issues, broken relationships, bankruptcy, foreclosure, etc. Following are a few ways that financial debt ruins your life:

It decreases the pleasure that you get out of life in several ways. First, you may not have any extra money to spend on eating out, entertainment and trips. Secondly, you might have to work long hours to pay your bills which will cut into your leisure time. Both of these scenarios results in a depressed attitude about life.

Stress causes many to become irritable and hard to get along with. Studies show that nothing stresses people out more than money worries. People who allow money problems to affect the way they treat their family are asking for trouble. Constant strife fractures the family, and a broken home may happen as a result.

Financial debt is like quicksand. It prevents you from ever getting ahead in life. And once you are in debt, it is extremely difficult to get out. The truth is that it is more expensive to live in debt than it is to live debt free. Interest payments are to blame. So, if you are in debt, you have less money because of those payments.

Fortunately, you don't have to let debt ruin your life. You can take steps that will change your life instantly. The first thing that you need to do is to stop buying things with credit. Adopt a simpler lifestyle until you can afford to pay cash for a better one.

Next, you may want to consider consolidating all of your bills into one loan with a low interest rate. This could save you a lot of money over the short and long term.

Lastly, you need to prioritize. Place your family and the things you enjoy at the top of the list. Work should only come after these things.

If you are happy in life, you will be more productive at work. Naturally, more money will follow. You don't have to work harder to get all of the things you want, you just have to learn how to get those things in a stress free, enjoyable way.

I recall a time when I received a telephone call from my friend Siegfried. For a long time he had been asking me if I would like to join him in business. I was happy and content moving along at my pace involved in the 'selling game'.

I had refused his offer many times because I was happy in my life as it was quiet and still below the 'Radar'. During this call it was different however, he asked for my help to train some of his sales people while he attended an unexpected event interstate. Little did I know it was a ploy to get me involved in business with him. This happened three weeks in a row. I was training his sales people for a new business venture he was starting.

Even though the business had me intrigued I was happy to hand him back the reins on his return. Here is the shock! It wasn't long after that I was sitting at my desk when I received some bad news. It was here I learned that my main income source at the time had to be "fire sold" and I was to be left with virtually nothing. Before receiving this news I believed I was a successful self-employed salesman.

When I heard the news I didn't really have any business to speak of at all. This may surprise some of you but you hear stories like that all the time.

It takes us all by surprise and even that this catastrophe had nothing to do with impropriety but was purely an internal matter within the business structure it was very devastating for me

When I lost that "golden opportunity" I had to start all over again. I sat around the house and contemplated how I was going to start earning an income and what I was going to do with my life.

But days turned into weeks, and before I knew it months had passed and I was still feeling more isolated and depressed by the day. In fact, I'm sure my parents were downright embarrassed. I was hitting rock bottom. If only things were different, maybe everything would be OK.

Over the next few years not being able to save, with my history and making some bad decisions I was building thousands of dollars of debt.

Then, just out of the blue, I recalled that devastating news that brought me so much heart ache and misery. After I sat there pondering the matter and after realising I couldn't retrieve much from dwelling on the past events I then suddenly had a warm feeling of comfort come over me.

The reason I clicked into a state of optimism rather than a state of depression again was because I knew I had the 'skills and know how' to get everything I had lost back within a short time. I thought 'there was now nothing stopping me from starting again except my state of mind'.

As I was planning my come back, guess who phoned me? Yes, it was Siegfried and yes it was time I finally took him up on his offer as a partner to join him in business. I knew I had the skills to make his and now my business into a bigger and better enterprise than I had ever done in business before. But I had to get out of debt and start saving...then apply all my knowledge.

The first step I used and what you will have to use in getting ahead and turning your life around is to get out of debt and start saving. I have collated the steps what worked for me in turning my life around and I've put them in this book for you.

Applying the Steps

They are all based on the lessons learned from the classic book: "The richest man in Babylon". My book is broken up into lessons. Each lesson is written as an email personally sent to you addressed to 'Robyn' giving you both the application and my experience in applying the techniques.

It's important that you access the links provided. They form part of the exercises in the book and will assist you in accomplishing your debt free goals. I hope you implement some of the ideas and enjoy the benefits of turning your situation around as much as I did.

The Ancient And Modern Wealth Formula

First of all... Congratulations! You've just made a smart decision about your financial future.

How so?

Because the advice I'm about to share with you is more than enough to change your financial situation beyond what you previously thought possible.

We'll start by getting you out of debt safely, and at the same time, I'll show how to start creating a large amount of spare money and wealth in your life.

And I want you to know something Robyn:

===========================
I've been there, done that!
===========================

It wasn't too long ago that I was in the same situation as you bordering on bankruptcy, faced with so many confusing crossroads and spending my most of precious years in downright misery, panic, anxiety and stress.

Most people say I'm now a multi-millionaire, and I have been helping others to follow my exact strategies to get themselves out of debt, and find more money in life too.

I'm not saying I can make you a millionaire. That's not really the goal here. The ultimate goal is to get you out of debt using the same system I used.

And not just out of debt, but reversing the process so that you actually start saving money and building a nest egg for you and your family.

The fact that I was able to do the same thing using these principles just goes to show you something no matter how bad things have gotten, there is always a way to get back on track, out of debt and even finding a way to create wealth in life.

However, I'm not here to assume I know everything about you. Because even though I know how it feels to be in your situation, I also understand that we all have our own unique situations too.

But here is what I do know:

==================
You CAN do this
==================

Whether you've tried and failed to solve your money problems or not whether you have big dreams or smaller daily financial goals I will show you how to get where you want to be, and fast.

How?

It's all thanks to a unique and proven formula for smashing your worst debt problems into pieces and helping you to bring life changing amounts of money into your world at the same time.

```
========================================
```
"Did you say there is a formula Dan?
What kind of formula?"
```
========================================
```

Well here's the thing. A few years ago, I was given a dusty old book called "The richest man in Babylon".

In this book, the author explained how any person - with the right information by their side could not only abolish their debt quickly, but also create an abundance of wealth in the process.

Naturally, I was both sceptical and hooked from the first page. As I gingerly dug into the book - both with doubt and excitement each page led me closer towards what I now consider my true saviour in life.

You see, as I got deeper into the book, it began to explain the key principles to getting out of debt and creating wealth, which were...

1. Fatten your wallet

2. Control expenditures

3. Make your assets multiply

4. Guard your assets from loss

5. Make a profitable investment

6. Insure a future income

7. Increase your ability to learn

Sounds simple doesn't it? Nothing revolutionary there, it seems. But there's more to it than that, and I'll explain why in just a second.

But for now, let me ask you... Do you at least AGREE with these principles?

Again, I can't promise you'll become an overnight millionaire simply by knowing those principles I just listed in fact, I can almost guarantee that simply "knowing" about those principles won't do much for you at all.

So why did I tell you them? And how did they help me make so much money whilst I was still young enough to enjoy it?

Well, I took those principles along with other nitty gritty details I unearthed in this dusty old book and formulated my own customized debt busting plan and as a result not only was I able to quickly crush my debt single handedly but I was also able to build multiple assets and streams of income at the same time.

Now I am going to show you how to do the same, just stick with me and you'll have all the answers you need. And before I leave you today, here's something I really need to remind you of:

```
============================
This WILL work for you, even if
the odds are stacked against you
============================
```

You see, I created wealth and escaped debt despite being broke, despite having no inheritance money, despite having no capital to invest and despite having no special friends to bail me out.

In other words, I did all this from the ground up - from the same position you're in now broke, stressed out, lost and confused.

So I can safely say that I will be able to do the same for you too. Because what I'm going to teach you is not conventional wisdom it doesn't rely on luck and it doesn't discriminate.

So Robyn, stick with me over the coming emails and I'll walk you through the entire process I used and now coach others with step by step.

But before you think "Sure, this might be great if I were some kind of business person or smart entrepreneur", then I have one last thing to say...

You do not need to be a business mogul, an entrepreneur, or a smart 'go getta' type for this system to work.

That's the beauty of the system; it works for anyone providing you can read basic English and are willing to actually put it into practice of course.

And for the record, I certainly wouldn't consider it "hard work" by the average 9-5 employee's standards. Heck, I also know that it doesn't take any special kind of intelligence to make this system work either.

So if you're smart and hardworking, you'll probably make a lot more than I did :

As we progress, you'll see why I can make such a claim.

```
=================================
```
Coming in your first lesson
```
=================================
```

I am going to share the first wealth building, debt-busting step with you.

This includes 7 questions you need to ask yourself about your current finances, how to find wealth in your own neighbourhood, and 4 practical steps to put it all into action immediately.

Stay tuned.

Dan Cavalli

P.S. - How does it feel to know that you're about to discover the secret to eliminating debt and finally be able to create multiple pay rises for yourself at will? It should make you buzz with excitement.

If it doesn't, I've got the wrong person. I want you to mark this day in your calendar it will be the day you look back on for the rest of your life, when you are telling your friends and family how you became so successful in life.

It makes me tingle being able to share this information and change people's lives, and it will make you tingle when you can look back and tell your life story with pride.

P.P.S - Please do not overlook this advice. It has been used by many large companies through to single parents... and everyone else in between. It's not complicated, it's not even hard work but boy, does it work.

In life you have two options...

Option 1: Work, work, work and cross your fingers that the government doesn't swallow up your hard earned pension funds when you decide to retire and rest for a few years before you sign out of this crazy world. Or...

Option 2: Handle your money wisely today, and find new ways to generate more money without working more hours. If you go with the second option, life begins to look a whole lot different for you.

You get to sleep at night, knowing you will never have to worry about sacrificing your kids' education

You will never have to worry about spending your last years in a retirement home. You will never have to skip holidays each year because the creditors hiked their interest rates and your boss won't give you a pay rise.

You also get to enjoy those precious summer holidays, walking across the beach with your lover or entire family smelling the salty air and Barbecue grill wafting across from the local restaurant, watching the sun set over the sea and hearing distant laughter from others who are as high on life as you are.

Without stressing over how much you can afford to spend during your trip, and without worrying how you'll pay for it all when you get home. You also get to surprise your partner or kids with those special birthday treats, and watch their face light up with admiration and joy towards you.

Again, without worrying about the interest rates you'll have to pay for the next ten years as a result. You get to move to a bigger home, where the kids have plenty of space, with a car on the driveway that gets the neighbourhood talking about you in a good way.

I could go on and on, but I'm sure you have your own ideas of what your ideal lifestyle would be like if you could only get some money, instead of being in debt and not earning enough, right?

Well, whatever that lifestyle may look like for you, that is exactly the kind of lifestyle that my advice and subsequent coaching will reward you with.

How do I know?

Because what I am going to be sharing with you are the same principles which made me a multi-millionaire and has helped countless other people escape debt and produce a level of wealth that is more than enough to support their dreams.

Whether YOUR dream means an extra holiday a year, or just a few extra grand per month, it's all possible with my help. I'll prove it to you and you'll see it for yourself as we progress together in these emails and next steps I have for you.

So, are you finally ready to start your pathway to your perfect new life for you and your loved ones? Great! So, the first thing we need to do - if we ever want that beach strolling, stress free, abundant lifestyle - is simply this:

===================
Know where to start!
===================

The first step in ridding debt and finding wealth is to assess your current financial situation. If you don't know where the bullets are flying in from, then there's no point running out into the battle field with a shotgun.

In other words, you need to do a quick self-assessment of where you are, and what you need to do first. This will help you to make a clear plan of action to find more money, protect yourself from losing more money, and grow your money at the same time.

=========================

Answer yes or no to the following questions:

1. Can I buy the food brands I want at the food checkout? YES/NO

2. Can I afford to pay for the expensive items? YES/NO

3. Can I give a gift of $3,000 to a friend without hurting? YES/NO

4. Can I stop my job and go on a holiday and not worry? YES/NO

5. Can I take my partner to an expensive restaurant and not worry about the bill? YES/NO

6. Can I give financial advice to a friend? YES/NO

7. Do my peers think I am well off? YES/NO

If your answers were predominantly NO, then we're on the right level, and you're the perfect candidate for my advice.

If you had a mix of answers, then you will still benefit from the advice I am going to be sharing with you, but we will need to tailor your plan accordingly.

Either way, the bottom line is this: Even if you answered "NO" to just one of the above, then there's clearly a financial strain going on in your life.

You see, just one "NO" indicates a crack in the framework just like how a dam bursts due to a small crack that has been there for years, your finances and life can burst apart at the seems just as easily. Even when it seems like nothing is at risk.

So now it's time for your practical assignment. Today, I want you to:

=======================
Seek out guidance and help
=======================

One of the quickest ways to get a proven result in life, is to emulate others who have already achieved that result. This is a proven fact in business, sport, and even in wars.

One person needs a result, so they simply "copy" what other winners have done. Simple, and saves you a lot of wasted time, money and energy.

So, here's what I want you to do... I want you to take a break from the routine, and go find out how others acquire wealth and free themselves of debt. In order for that to happen, I want you to do the following exercise:

1. Buy a financial diary $3 - $5 from a news agency or book store.

2. Ask yourself do I know more than 3 rich people? If not find 3 people from associates, newspaper, yellow pages or ask your accountant, doctor or dentist and record their name and contact details in your financial diary.

3. Make contact with all three and ask at least one who is willing to meet you for a cup of coffee.

4. Ask them at the coffee shop how they got started on their journey to wealth and to give you advice how to do the same.

Don't expect all the answers to come at once. Make this an ongoing investigation. Look at it like a fun hobby, don't take yourself too seriously.

Play detective and find out what other folks are doing, in your neighbourhood, in your country, or globally you'll see patterns. Those patterns will unlock a lot of doors for you.

```
==============================
```
There are three reasons why I need you to
do this exercise:
```
==============================
```

1. It will show you how a wide range of people can make a lot of money, not just smart or privileged folks

2. It will show you what steps you need to take to begin building wealth, based on your current situation (we're not talking about starting the next Microsoft here)

3. It will allow you to build your network - because the more rich people you have in your address book, the more opportunities will arise when you are ready

These things might seem alien at first. You might think you can skip this step. But I assure you, this is a very important step. You must get out there and find out what people are doing to make money. It's easier than you might think too, because these people can't wait to share their stories.

This will give you all kinds of ideas, plus new level of hope and inspiration too. This is just as much about mind-set building, as it is about getting practical advice from people who have been there and done it.

And remember, if you ever want to get out of debt and build a better future for you and your family, then creating more income without working overtime at the office is one of the fastest and most liberating ways to do so.

In the next lesson, I want to start locking down on your debt. I'll be showing you how to start an effective savings plan, how to set money saving targets you really can stick to, and how to save money without even noticing or thinking about it.

That's just the start of a whole lot more advice I have for you, so stay tuned and don't miss a single email so stay tuned,

Dan Cavalli

I want to tackle your debt

In this email, I want to tackle your debt. After all, it's hard to create wealth when all your cash is being siphoned off to some greedy credit card company or banker each month.

There are basically 2 obvious ways to get out of debt:

1. Save more money
(cutting interest rates, saving money at home, controlling spending etc)

2. Make more money
(finding out how to generate passive income, new opportunities, investments etc)

Today, I want to start somewhere simple where you can immediately take action and actually start to see results in the next few days and weeks.

```
========================
```
Saving money
```
========================
```

In that old dusty book I read a few years ago the book that has made many millionaires and saved many people from debt, including myself, it contained one key principle which was to "Plant the seeds of success"

In my '24 week' coaching program, I incorporate this principle as early on as Possible (more details about that later). Starting your journey to financial freedom is much easier if you start saving money first.

Once you are able to save money, you have options. You have room to breathe, and something to fall back on in case of emergencies. Without savings, you have no option but to live in confinement. You also have no safety net, and you'll always be forced to hit the credit cards and loans when an emergency arises and that just piles on more debt in the future, like a costly downward spiral.

That's why it's so important to apply this step correctly and as fast as you possibly can. Trust me, it will put you in good stead for everything I want to help you with in the coming weeks and months.

So, how do you start saving? Usually, folks find saving difficult and see it as some sort of sacrifice, but it doesn't have to be that way for you. The first thing you need to keep on track is a savings plan.

In order to start a successful savings plan, you need to work out what your bills are and how much you can save comfortably. Don't worry, you only need to do this once, and the resulting benefits will soon become very obvious to you.

For this step I advise you to get your goals and planning system from this website link below:

http://www.the-richest-man-in-babylon.com/docs/goals.doc

Important: Once you have that document, I only want you to complete the first financial page nothing else.

You will find this plan extremely useful for getting a clear picture of your finances, and making sense of where you are, and where you need to be.

Trust me, the simple process of writing it all out in this structured plan will take a huge mental weight off your mind which will help clear your head and allow you to sleep a little better a night.

But it does much more than that, It gives you specific, realistic goals. And that's important, because all success in this world comes from well planned Goals from athletes to traders, astronauts to dieters.

I could give you dozens of famous quotes about planning and effective goals, but I think you're smart enough to agree with this already, right? If you need more detailed planning, I have also found an advanced savings planner that you can use: http://bit.ly/undermoney

Money is grown from money. If you don't have any to start with, that's where you stay broke. It doesn't matter what the amount is, just save some so that you are planting seeds to breed success.

=================
What next?
=================

Now that you have everything planned out, you will know your targets and how much you ideally need to save. Even if you're not sure how much to save, you must start saving something today.

This is a crucial part of the debt busting and wealth building Plan so please make sure you follow this through before the next lesson!

Speaking of which, the next lesson contains specific steps you can take to save even more money which should be useful to you, now that you have a plan in place.

Stay tuned.

Dan Cavalli

Money is grown from money

In the last email, I gave you a savings plan worksheet for you to fill in. That should have given you a better idea of where you are, and where you need to be.

Remember, saving is a crucial step in wealth creation, and it's also a very smart way to protect yourself from emergencies and further borrowing.

And not just that, but savings are an asset which will allow you to grow your finances, instead of paying some greedy banker all your wages.

After all, money is grown from money. If you don't have any to start with, then that's where you stay… broke. It doesn't matter what the amount is, but what does matter is that you save at least some of your income. This way, you'll be planting the seeds for your inevitable success.

But I admit, it's not always easy to save money when you don't have much spare income to save in the first place. Again, remember that you only need to save what you can afford to save.

Be ruthless, but remain realistic too. Otherwise you'll end up shooting yourself in the foot. Even if you can only save $1 per week, you're doing good and making a difference.

What you have to remember is, money makes money. You may START with saving $1 per week, but if you follow my advice, you'll quickly see that money grow like a rose bush in the spring.

=========================
If self-discipline is a problem
=========================

If you're struggling with the whole self-discipline thing (which we all do from time to time) then here's a tip:

Set up a direct deposit into a savings account, or go one step further and ask your accountant/boss/partner to deduct the money from your pay slip before it hits your bank account.

Sometimes it's easier to do this, because it removes temptation, and is one less thing to handle or think about in the first place. You may notice a slight change at first, but you'll adapt quickly and if it means you have one less coffee per day in order to build your nest-egg, can you really justify giving up so easily.

Of course not, you're stronger than that, right? So in summary, here are a couple of things you should do when starting your savings plan:

1. Open a new savings account with your bank. It is to be used for saving only.

2. Ask your current employer to deduct a small amount (say 5% of your weekly salary) and deposit it into your savings account.

That's all there is to it. Later on, you'll see how this small savings commitment will empower you, give you confidence, and become the seed of something much bigger. But let's not jump the gun, we're still finding our feet.

==============
What's next?
==============

The next email will help you take another crucial step in the right direction, where I will explain how you can expand on today's lesson to manage your debt and bill payments much more easily.

The result? You never miss a payment, never get charged for missed payments, and you'll be able to start repairing your credit history as a result.

Again, stuff you really cannot afford to miss.

Stay tuned,

Dan Cavalli

Temptations and hassles

Ok, in the last email I talked about setting up automatic deposits from your pay check into a savings account, to handle your savings and remove the temptations and hassles from the equation.

Today is a simple expansion of that technique, why not do the same for your creditors and bills? After all, a lot of the problems with bills and debts is managing them and paying them on time, right?

Heck, even with a direct debit set up, we can often overshoot the budget and not have enough money to pay those bills and debts each month.

But whenever that happens, you get a black mark against your name, and your home (in most countries) which damages your credit score for anyone living under your roof.

So that's why it is vital that you manage your payments for creditors and bills. Plus, the more automated your payments are, the less thinking and paperwork is required.

Win win!

So, to automate the process and make sure you never miss a payment for bills or creditors, there's two things you need to do: 1. Work out how much your monthly bills amount to (convert it to weekly to match your pay period)

2. Ask your current employer to deduct your monthly bills dollar value and deposit it into a new "Bills" account.

3. Set up a direct debit from that account to pay all your bills and creditors on time.

This may seem obvious, and possibly close to what many folks already do, but the difference is that most people set up a direct debit from their current/main account and usually at the end of the month.

What the problem with that? Well, it can be hard to control cash flow in a single main account, with so many things flying in and out of it all month. And secondly, you run the risk of running out of cash before the bills are due.

With a second account that siphons off the exact amount of money needed before it lands in your main account, things become much clearer from the first day of the month, and you never have to stress or worry about the bills being paid or not because it's already taken care of, automatically.

====================
What's next?
====================

Ever wondered why some people seem to always fall into money, and others don't? It's not always the dumb luck you might assume it is.

I'll prove it to you.

Stay tuned,

Dan Cavalli

Secret to getting rich

What is the secret to getting rich? I've found that it is so simple, that almost everybody overlooks it. People are looking for the answers that they think are so complex that only a few wise men and women could possibly have the answer.

The truth is, making money is often a lot more simple and systematic than you are led to believe. Sure, we are not all stock traders, world class experts, movie stars, or the next Bill Gates but the great thing is, you don't have to be.

There is so much abundance of wealth in this world, with so many people buying, selling and creating trade that it allows the average person a chance to take a slice of the pie too.

You don't need to own an award winning business or have a background in business school to make money, you don't even need to be in business at all. There are just so many ways to create wealth, and often it starts with what you have already got.

That's the beauty of this world you can take what you've got and turn it into more of the same, or something far bigger and better, far quicker than you can work for it at the 9-5 office job.

But before you can start making smart decisions with your money and turning what you have into what others wish they had, we need to take a step back for a moment.

You see, I truly believe based on personal experience and from studying many other successful people in this world that the only way to free your-self of debt and start creating wealth at the same time is to have the right mind-set in place first.

A positive mind-set towards money, knowing why you want money in the first place will drastically speed up the process and keep you glued to your goals long after the dust has settled.

And by working on your mind-set and motivations for money, you may get a few surprises too.

For example, you may actually find that you don't need as much money as you think you do or you may find a real emotional reason for getting all the money you can dream of, which will be a vital driving force in the upcom-ing lessons and coaching I have for you.

Either way, you cannot make your fortune until you know the real reason why you want money, and until you can look at money objectively and with a healthy attitude towards it.

```
===========================
```
The bottom line is this:
```
===========================
```

Those that become rich have a core desire that they have tapped into. Those that handle money well, all have a positive attitude towards money.

These are the two things you need, otherwise you're simply building your fortress on quick sand.

Stay tuned,

Dan Cavalli

Email seven:

Tap into these things inside of you

In this lesson, I need to tap into these things inside of you. Otherwise, nothing from this point onwards will actually work. So, your action today is to complete the following questions. There is no right or wrong answers and if you can't answer any question just think about them for a while.

Print this email and keep this sheet below for your diary and for a record of your personal growth through this course:

=====================

Date: "Count my Blessings Chart"

What is it that makes me feel my life is already full of riches?
What makes me feel great?
What makes me feel like I'm a millionaire?
What do I give to show my appreciation?
What can I do to show my appreciation?
What can I do to practice feeling more like I have an abundance of riches?

=====================

Don't rush this one. Take your time and be honest with yourself. Remember, this isn't a trick question kind of thing, it's about getting into the right mind-set about money and wealth. It won't happen overnight, so save it, print off copies, and return to it.

Trust me, this is not "positive thinking mumbo jumbo" this is a crucial part of the training, which fuels everything you have done and will be doing from here on out. Remember, wealth comes from the mind first the practical stuff is the easy part.

===================
What's next?
===================

The next lesson is going to expand on this a bit more, and I have another set of questions attacking from a different angle.

This will help you identify any old thinking habits towards money (or your lack of it), so please make sure you open the email and take action.

I'll see you on the next lesson,

Stay tuned,

Dan Cavalli

Your way to a wealthy lifestyle

Before I begin today's email, I want to congratulate you once more. We're already finished lesson 7, clearly, that shows me you are dedicated enough to truly rid your debt and find your way to a wealthy lifestyle.

But whilst many folks are taking this same journey with you Robyn, it is also sad to admit that a small minority of folks simply gave up a few emails back for what could have been a number of reasons.

==========================
But you're different, you've got what it takes.
==========================

I can already tell. And trust me, thanks to the momentum of everything you've done so far, it gets easier and easier to shatter debt and start building wealth from this point.

But we are not quite done yet, there's still more things to put into action to really get that debt shrinking and begin generating noticeable wealth.

In the last email, you will recall the exercise I asked you to do which got you thinking about money, and happiness in life, right? Make no mistake, that exercise was not filler or fluff. It was strategically placed in this series of emails to help you establish a good mind-set towards money.

And if you remember, I also explained why this is so important...

```
==========================================
```
Because nobody apart from lottery winners
can create wealth if they don't know why they want it.
```
==========================================
```

Sure, people who fall into a lot of money might live a year or three going crazy but they have not prepared themselves emotionally or practically.

They begin to struggle with money management. They begin to feel guilty for not knowing what to do with the money. They begin to lose sight of the value of small change.

They see money as a toy, and no longer important. But they spend, Spend, spend! Not realizing that the money won't last forever. It's really sad to see it, but it's true.

If only they treated money with healthy regard, instead of spending it like it was going out of fashion. If only they knew how to handle their money and make it work for them.

This is the same for anyone who finds money in life, but is mentally unprepared for it. Everyone assumes that money creates an easy life. Sure, it does but only if you know how to handle the beast.

Spending habits, negative associations, personal traits they can all shake you off your horse without you seeing the hurdle coming at you at 50 miles per hour.

So, I can stress how important it is for you and me to drill a bit deeper into this mind-set stuff, before I start setting you up with the big bucks.

I want you to do a similar exercise as the last email gave you, but this one is a little different but equally important. Just like last time, there are no right or wrong answers and if you can't answer any question just think about them for a while.

This exercise is designed to reveal what you really think of money. Answer truthfully to get the most from this exercise. Keep it as a record of personal growth through this course.

So, go ahead and print out the following exercise and complete the following questions:

"The Money And Me Chart"

1. Money is

_____
_____

2. The rich are

_____
___

3. My biggest fear about money is

_____

4. Money can make people

_____

5. If I had money I could

_____

6. I would have more money if

_____

7. I think money

_____

8. I was taught that money

_____

9. Money is the blame for

_____

10. To get more money I would have to

_____

11. If I had more money I'm afraid I

_____

Remember why this is important: Any negative thoughts even if they are true to you are hindering your journey to creating wealth. Do these exercises every day until your real feelings about money come out. If it is negative it must be eliminated.

And yes, we'll learn how to eliminate negative thoughts towards money very soon, but for now, all I want you to do is simply identify them. Be honest, because the only person you can cheat is yourself with this!

====================
What's coming up next?
====================

In the next email, we'll be covering a more practical aspect of this training, which involves the first crucial step to actually building your money, instead of just saving and managing it.

Stay tuned,

Dan Cavalli

Key wealth building principles

One of the key wealth building principles that will take an average earning employee to a higher social status and income bracket, has nothing to do with getting a better job or relying on savings instead, it is when that person decides to invest in something with a sure-fire return.

If you've been following my advice so far, then you'll already be building a nice savings account which you can grow, by making safe investments.

That means you don't have to change anything new in your current spending habits which should help you feel at ease, and won't create any risk.

But the problem is, what do you invest in? How much and where? What is safe, what is too risky?

I'm not going to give you some kind of tip off in this email, because it would devalue it (considering there are a lot of people reading this email at the same time as you).

But here's what I will advise you to do:

```
=====================================
```
Get advice from a financial expert
```
=====================================
```

Maybe from one of your wealthy associates you had a meeting with in your first lesson?

Seek a personal recommendation, or an acclaimed expert with lots of credentials. Take your time and hunt down a few, and find out a little more about them.

These people are your first gateway to growing your planted seeds from the savings we've been building until now. Make no mistake, this is a universally effective, non-discriminate way to your own financial independence.

We're not looking to make a quick risky buck here. Your investments will be verified, and on good authority (from your advisers).

The category of investments will be determined by your present situation. Again, this is why a financial coach or financial advisor will be invaluable to you, because they can determine the best course of action based on your personal circumstances.

```
==============================
```
So, here's what I need you to do today:
```
==============================
```

1. Find two banks or financial planning organisations that will give free advice about financial planning.

2. Make an appointment with 2 financial planners (for education purposes only do not act upon their advice yet).

This will set you up for this crucial investing stage. Don't panic, you won't be putting all your money on stocks (bad idea at the best of times). You won't be risking your home, or any assets (and no good adviser would tell you to anyway).

I want you to set up your first small investment with the help of your financial advisor. Don't let them talk you into big shiny promises. Simply take a small portion of your savings and insist that's all you have to invest.

Don't be tempted to get carried away. This is all about taking small steps at this stage, because the real wealth building comes later on, where I have a specific set of instructions for you (which build upon these introductory emails).

=================================
Coming up in the next email
=================================

I want to show you:

1. How you can improve your financial situation without receiving a single dollar more in income.

2. Why pay rises make no difference to our wealth

3. How to give yourself a pay rise, without working harder or longer hours

All of this is another crucial addition to your training so far. You have come a long way already.

-Learning how to save,

-How to improve your attitude towards money,

-How to manage money,

-Even how to start making your savings grow at a rapid rate

But I still have even more money-building, debt-busting tricks up my sleeve and the next email comes loaded with one of the easiest of them all.

Stay tuned,

Dan Cavalli

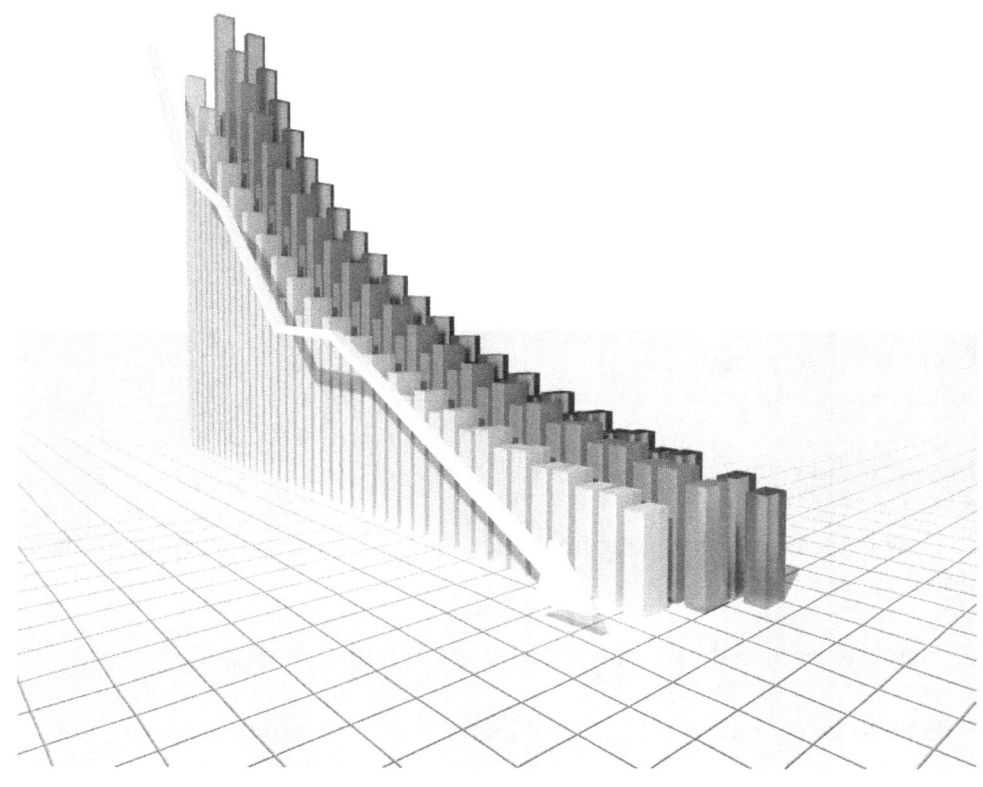

Five key areas where your money is hurting

There are five key areas where your money is hurting you, instead of setting you free. These are areas in your life that are swallowing up your hard earned money, for no reason or need at all.

The companies associated with these areas of your spending know this all too well, and they are smiling from ear to ear as your money is regularly transferred from your bank account to theirs, without you even noticing.

So let's shine a light on these money holes, and plug the leaks so that this money gets diverted back into your bank account and into your savings pot instead of someone else's, ok?

Some of them we've talked about, but need a strong reminder. Others are less obvious, but still need your attention.

===================
Here they are...
===================

1. Debt

Consolidate debts as soon as possible...as in this afternoon. It's not complicated these days, especially with all the online tools available. You can do
this in one sitting with most companies.

If you have credit cards, finance or personal loans consolidate them into
one loan and throw away your credit card if you don't have the discipline
to pay it off during the credit free period. Depending on your situation you
could save as much as $50 a week.

2. Hobbies and Leisure time.

Don't let your hobby become your nemesis. Some people fail to achieve
financial success because they have an interest that consumes all their time
and most of their money. The most important thing to note is that it takes
up your time. Time is money and you have a choice in how you want to
use it, either by spending it on too much pleasure or working towards your
future financial goals.

Time is like a cheque book. You only have so many cheques to tear
out of the butt until your money is gone. Once they have been used
there is no more money [or time as in this case].

But you don't have to be a miser and go too far. Just start where
you spend on those little wasters and work your way up the list.
The challenge is to look for a hobby or leisure activity that you
enjoy but one that will produce an income. Just think what you
could do if you had another 3 hours a day to produce an income. You
target savings here should be around $50 a week.

3. Luxuries.

The simplest and easiest way is to start from home. At work commit not to
buy any food outside what can be brought from home. That includes food

bought, smoko's, morning teas and lunches from restaurants, cafes or take away shops.

You can go further to cut costs by reducing your cigarette intake and shopping for specials. Same goes for all the other time wasters like television, excessive sleeping, sport etc. But you don't have to be a miser and go too far. Just start where you spend on those little wasters like I've mentioned. Your target savings here should be around $40 a week.

4. Insurance.

Only a fool doesn't protect their assets. But a fool pays for it when it's not needed. There are a number of ways to reduce the cost of insurance. The 'excess' is the main culprit.

Wearing a larger 'excess' up front could halve your insurance costs. Although this would not cover you for a small cost it would cover you for a serious loss.

Be prepared to pay for the small costs yourself and you'll find the premium will reduce accordingly. For the person who doesn't want to rip off the insurance companies with small and illegitimate claims this is an excellent way to save money.

Hire a broker as they are a free resource. The insurance companies pay for their time. I've pooled my insurance policies and have saved up to 40% on premiums. Your target savings here should be around $20 a week.

5. Electricity.

There is plenty of evidence to show that up to two thirds of household energy consumption is wasted. Check with your providers to see if you can do anything on your bills.

You can save as much as 37%. Get a energy consultant to inspect your whole energy spend for your household. Some councils do this for almost free, so ask.

The key here in this section is all about moderation, not instant gratification. Don't throw away your hard earned money because it's too hard to come by.

```
=========================
```
Today's goal for you...
```
=========================
```

Your action today is to list the amount of money you believe you can save per week from following the suggestions above.

1. Consolidate debts

2. Hobbies and Leisure time

3. Luxuries

4. Insurance

5. Electricity

Again, please do not skip this step. Every single penny you can find from each of these places in your life will add up quickly, and can make a drastic addition to your weekly and monthly savings pot.

I'll be back in a jiffy,

Stay tuned,

Dan Cavalli

How much we earn in our jobs

Why is it that no matter how much we earn in our jobs, it never seems to be enough?

Sure, we continue to work hard, work longer hours and get more money, but wouldn't it be nice if we could make money without begging the boss for a raise, or staying late at the office or factory every night?

Not only is it possible, but it's fundamental in your training with me. You see, it really is possible to improve your financial situation without receiving a single dollar more in income.

And that means you can save more, invest more, and enjoy more of your money as a result. That's what this is all about isn't it? Giving yourself more chances to spend money and grow your money without handing it all over to the creditors, right?

Listen, the truth is there are many professionals, doctors, lawyers and

Others who earn high incomes but are paupers, always struggling for more money. Clearly, it isn't an income problem but rather what is being done with the money.

Let me share an example with you: If you were to reduce your costs by $7 a day and banked that for a return of around 10% [this will vary with each economic climate] within 5 years that would have grown to $44,000 and within 27 years it would have grown to $350,000.

At that point you could have invested it into a block of flats and lived off the rental investment. All for the measly sum of $7 a day. The bottom line is this:

Your savings are the seed for your financial growth, they are not just "spare cash for a rainy day". Please remember that, it's very important.

You see, with savings, you can leverage your income and options more than it may appear on the surface. For example...

1. $100 saved has more power than a $100 pay rise because you are leaving out the tax man. If you were to cut your spending by $200 a week and were on a 49% tax bracket you would be in the same position as if you received a $20,000 annual pay increase.

2. Keeping the same tax rate and the $200 a week savings scenario, it is the same as having $170,000 invested at 12%.

All of a sudden saving $200 puts a different light on the subject doesn't it?

===================
Today's task
===================

So with that in mind, your goal today is to list 4 ways you think you can save $10.00 week:

1. _____

2. _____

3. _____

4. _____

This step is crucial. The more you can add to your savings stash, the quicker your money will grow for you, and the more doors will open up to you in the near future.

As you can see from the examples above, you don't need to beg your boss for a pay rise or work overtime all week to start building wealth.

===================
Coming up next...
===================

In the next email, I want to show you how to find "hidden money". It is money that is technically and legally yours, but is hiding in many systems surrounding you (usually at the benefit of others, and at your sheer expense).

Look out for that email, it's another big step in adding more money to your savings and investment pile. And remember, the more of that you have, the more you can multiply your money in smart investments going forward.

Stay tuned,

Dan Cavalli

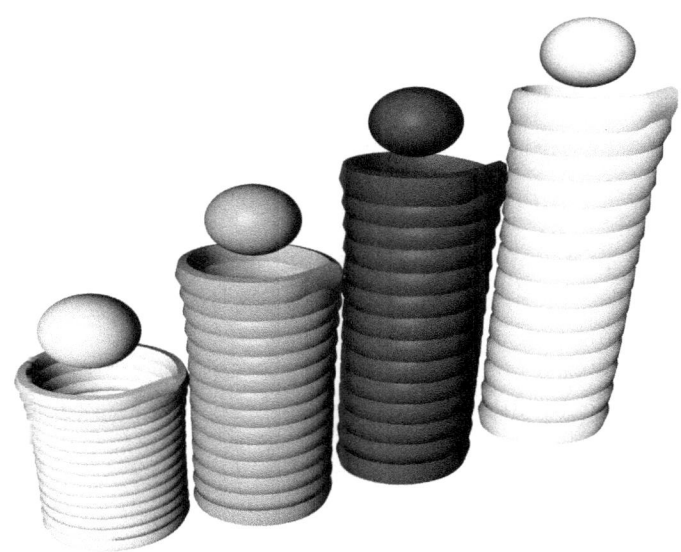

What you will have achieved

Once again, congratulations are in order. Well done, you've stuck with me long enough to discover just some of the core principles and actions steps you needed to know, in order to start reversing your debt and creating wealth in your life.

Sure, it's a steady process at first and I don't promise millions overnight. But if you've put my goals and pieces of advice into action, then here's what you will have achieved:

- You will know exactly where you are financially, and what needs to be done to get back on track

- You will have a realistic and clear savings plan to stick to

- You will have learned how to avoid self-discipline issues

- You will have set up your accounts to avoid charges and money management problems

- You will have developed a healthy attitude towards money, and a true meaningful reason for working hard to get it (this will drive you for the rest of your life)

- You will have found outside help for growing your nest egg and protecting your money

- You will finally know how to save small amounts each week and month, and generate a large income from these savings (without needed to switch jobs or work harder)

- You will know how to plug 5 major money leaks in your life, without making life dull

So what's next? What about furthering your education!

Well, the things you've learned so far are a fantastic start to your debt busting, wealth creating journey. I created these lessons to give you something real that you can put into action by yourself.

I wanted you to have the feeling of self-confidence and empowerment to finally take back control of your life, with a gentle nudge and point in the right direction from me.

Now that you have the early stages set up, with your planning sheets and personal experiences and thoughts documents, I would like to invite you to take the next step and enrol in my very limited debt elimination and wealth building program.

This is a program which is custom made around you, based on your current situation and the things you have documented in the previous tasks.

Here's the full scoop at: http://www.trmib.com/coaching The coaching program is designed to get you out of debt and creating substantial amounts of money through smart money management, investing, opportunities and personal development.

I'll personally guide you through each of these areas in a way that takes the pressure off you, so it becomes a case of simply following my lead and taking each weekly step as it comes, to get real results.

There are many benefits of this coaching program, along with some very important reasons why I truly believe this will help somebody in your situation, Robyn. So take 5 minutes right now, and see why: http://www.trmib.com/coaching.

I'll cover some more about my optional coaching course in the next email.

Stay tuned,

Dan Cavalli

P.S - As you'll see, this coaching program is not only affordable, but is guaranteed to make you more money than you currently have…a lot more. If it doesn't, you don't pay a penny for my personal time, ever.

An interesting little story for you today

I have an interesting little story for you today, with a very important message at the end of it.

During the war, a squadron leader led his troops deep down into an enemy bunker. In this bunker was a huge vault containing priceless possessions, maps, and other intelligence.

Infiltrating the vault would surely win the war, and make the soldiers both famous and wealthy when they returned home. As the troops reached the vault, they were confronted with a huge steel door, several feet high.

```
==============================
Exhausted, they gave up...
==============================
```

After many attempts to ram or blow up the door, the troops collapsed in an exhausted heap.

The squadron leader gathered his men in a line. "Which of you men can think of another way to penetrate this steel door?" He asked with authority.

Many of the troops shook their heads, some examined the door's dimensions and weight trying to calculate things like mass and leverage points to prize the door open. But none of their theories made enough sense, or were humanly possible for these tired, injured troops.

As some of the more educated, influential men in the squadron finally admitted that it was an impossible task, other fellow troops quickly followed suit.

```
===============================
```
Apart from one quiet soldier
```
===============================
```

Apart from one quiet soldier, who approached the door with a sense of calm and reason. He tapped the steel door, assessed it's width and depth, looked at the hinges and began running his hands over the steel surface.

Finally, he made his decision. After a deep breath, he centred himself and pulled gently on the huge steel vault door. It swung open easily, effortlessly and freely. "It must have be jammed or something" the onlooking troops baulked.

But that was not the case. In fact, the steel door had actually been left slightly ajar, and the design was so precise that only the slight touch was required to open it and too much force would cause it to jam into the frame of the wall.

```
===============================
```
"A valuable lesson..."
```
===============================
```

The squadron leader turned to his other troops and said: "Today you have learned a valuable lesson, men."

"Which is what?" They replied.

"Today you have learned that in order to get what you want out of a situation, you need five things.

First, you need to open your eyes and see the problem for what it really is.

Secondly, you must never make false assumptions.

Thirdly, you must be willing to make a decision.

Fourth, you must have the courage to act with boldness and conviction.

And finally, never be afraid to make mistakes"

==
How this relates to YOU, Robyn
==

You might be wondering what this has to do with your financial situation, your debt, and your chances of creating truth wealth?

Well, in the previous emails I have shown you how to assess your situation and see your problem for what it really is. This helps you to get a grip on where you are and what needs to be done to solve the debt (and find more money in your life).

Next, it's easy to make false assumptions about clearing your debt and making a lot of money in life.

It's not your fault most people are born and raised to believe that the only way to eliminate debt and create wealth is through being lucky, or being friends with certain people, or being really smart, or whatever else has been drummed into you for so many years.

But just like the solider who didn't assume the steel vault door couldn't be opened, if you can put aside old assumptions for long enough, I'll show you how to get all the money you could ever imagine in your life.

==
You just need to know where to look,
and what to do when you see "it".
==

More about my coaching option for you to consider (I am not pushing my services) but I'd like to welcome you (as an existing customer) into my personal coaching program, where we will take everything you have learned so far, along with all of the plans and exercise sheets you've carefully filled out, and begin to put the money making wheels in motion.

When you begin your coaching with me, you'll literally be taken by the hand and shown exactly how to start accelerating your savings, our income and your investments in a way that defies conventional knowledge.

And the best part is, you won't pay a penny for my time. To see why, and learn more about this rare and very unique coaching opportunity, please visit: http://www.trmib.com/coaching.

A special discount applies ($47 instead of $89) for customers reading this book. Just send me an email that you are a reader and I'll make sure you get it at the $47.

If you see a large "closed" message when you arrive at the website, then I'm afraid the best I can offer you is to be placed on the 6 month waiting list until new spots open up. Unfortunately it always fills up fast, so take 5 minutes right now to learn what the coaching offers.

The bottom line is, if you choose to accept that there's only one answer or solution to a situation/question/problem then you'll only ever give and get the same result.

That is, until someone can come along and show you that there are less conventional ways to solve common problems - such as debt and limitations on the money you are making right now.

Stay tuned

Dan Cavalli

P.S - Of course, there's a reason why most people remain in debt, and are left baffled at the possibility of making a fortune in life because we're brought up being told the same thing "Work hard, be grateful for what you have and accept that."

Be grateful for what you have

Whilst that's a good mantra, it's not the same mantra that financially wealthy people live and die by. Sure, they work hard, but there's a limit to how hard you can work and how many hours you have in the day. You'll struggle to make a million per year simply by doing overtime every night, or even getting a promotion after 5 years.

And sure, you should be grateful for what you have but does that mean you have to stay where you are in life? What's wrong with reaching for the stars?

Simply put, if you choose to live life the way others expect you to, then you'll always have an average life at best. It's not a personal trait, it's simply a lack of knowledge and guidance in life.

Births, weddings, funerals, holidays, health care...it's no wonder we find ourselves in large amounts of debt. But the problem is, most of us never escape it, let alone build assets or other streams of income.

Getting rich remains a dream heck, even getting out of debt is a fantasy for most of us. In the UK alone, 80% of debt is secured against people's homes, with more than 44% of people looking for professional help and guidance.

In the US, the average household credit card debt is $15,000. People are losing homes to foreclosure, jobs aren't paying enough for modern and comfortable living, education and health costs are continually rising and then there's the pension to think about, your kid's wedding, rising fuel costs. Let's face it, life ain't cheap and it certainly ain't getting cheaper.

But does that mean you have to lie down and take it? Clearly, by the very fact that you've hung on with me this far, you're not willing to back down and let money control you anymore. You're not ready to join the legions of divorcees who let money prize their love and family apart.

You're not ready to ruin your health through lack of sleep and endless nights of stress and anxiety over bills and debt. You're not ready to spend the rest of your life working like a dog, only to be rewarded with just enough money to pay the bills and the rising interest rates on that growing pile of debt.

You're not ready to spend your best days of your life, feeling guilty over what you buy, what you can't afford to buy for others.....or ashamed and embarrassed, jealous and frustrated that the Jones' family next door have the car, the holidays and the healthy well educated kids that you deserve too.

You're sick and tired of facing this kind of future, despite the fact that you work hard and try to live a good honest life, setting a good example to your family.

I know how it feels, and just like you, I took real action to do something about it. All it requires are simple, proven steps and you can begin to see your debt dwindle, and your assets grow within just a few weeks no matter how bad things have gotten for you.

You have already taken the first step by signing up for this email course, but the next step is where the really big changes begin to happen and far more quickly too.

Stay tuned

Dan Cavalli

How you got into debt

I really don't care why or how you got into debt. It really is none of my business.

I have no business in judging others, as I was once crushed by debt myself. It's an easy trap to fall into, but not so easy to climb out of, as I'm sure you know too well.

But what I do have a business in saying, is how you can get out of debt, and how you can actually reverse the process so dramatically, that you actually begin to accumulate wealth instead.

But before you even stand a chance of that, let's take a look at some of the reasons why you are finding it so hard to get out of debt the traditional way...

1. It can be confusing and time consuming trying to fix debt alone.

2. Your debt grows like a weed, cutting off your air supply until you reach a point where saving money seems impossible.

3. Your current boss won't give you a pay rise, or you can't find a better paid job right now.

4. You don't want to risk your money trying to make money, and gambling is not something you consider fun.

5. A lot of financial aids and counsellors don't actually walk the walk, cost a lot of money that you really cannot afford, and don't come with any guarantees.

Stay tuned,

Dan Cavalli

P.S - As I previously mentioned, a lot of financial aids and counselling is provided by people who have no idea what true wealth is, or how it can be obtained. Sure, they may show you how to reduce your debts, or cheat the system, or risk money for some kind of gain, but is that what you really want?

How to break free from debt

You know, most people assume the reason they can't get out of debt
is because of high interest rates, or not being able to afford to pay off the
debt quickly enough (if at all).

And yes, those are big reasons, but there's more to it than that. You see,
creditors know that there are lots of ways to keep you in debt, and even
more reasons why you'll never get out of debt alone, or alive.

Debt counselling companies are one of those reasons. You know, it's hard
to make it through a single commercial break these days, without some
cheesy guy offering some kind of debt consolidation program for you to
try.

The problem is, despite the bold claims and promises, the truth is that debt
counselling services are really just a fancy term for a repayment plan over a
long time.

They work by negotiating with your creditors to lower your interest Charges but in the process, you get lumped into a repayment plan, which poten-
tially drags on like a thorn in your side, for several years.

Worse still, they require a large payment and fees to use them...often with
no money back guarantee at the end of it. Not my idea of smart money-
building.

I'm not saying these services never work, because sometimes they do but
the statistics show that most of them backfire and waste both your time
and your money.

Stay tuned,

Dan Cavalli

You can't always do it all by yourself

When you're in debt, sooner or later there are two questions that you end up asking:

1. What do I do now?

2. Who can I turn to?

You know you can't always do it all by yourself, because things like self-discipline, old spending habits, lack of time, lack of experience all end up getting in your way.

It's easy to let life's distractions take over and end up burying your head in the sand. But you have clearly woken up to your reality, because otherwise you wouldn't be reading this email.

I really am not surprised why people remain in debt, let alone find it impossible to build assets and wealth in life. After all, there's one expense after the other, and so many personal issues which get in the way.

Bankers, lenders and credit card companies know this all too well. That's why they lend you the money. BECAUSE they know you'll pay them over and over and over, paying back more than you actually borrowed in the first place.

They send their shiny new credit cards to 18 year old kids in the mail these days and it's like taking candy from a baby.

They prey on your desperate situations and deep desires to lure you into their spider web of debt.

Listen, don't kid yourself these companies only exist and grow by taking more of your money, more of the time and that's exactly why I believe you need something drastically different to save you from this situation.

So that's why the next part of the book 'The Richest Man in Babylon' excited me even more, as I discovered how to actually build assets and wealth.

Section 2 - The wealth building principles of that dusty old book.

1. Start filling your bag from every 10 coins you earn, spend only nine of them. You will see how your bag starts filling quickly. You will see what else you can do with this spare income, so you can be earning money quickly.

2. Control your "obligatory expenses" that grow in proportion to your income, and avoid confusing desire with needs.

3. Make your gold multiply - Make your gold work for you, then its son's [interest] and the sons of their sons. Investing your gold through loans and opportunities. Gold multiplies fast.

4. Protect your gold from any lost if you have got gold, you will be tempted to invest in any attractive project. Assure your capital. Its not true romantics make a fast fortune. Ask the wise people about what they know.

5. Make your property a rental investment - If you can eat grapes from your

vineyard and have a nice house it inspires you to finish your duties.

6. Assure future incomes foresee some incomes for your old age and your family. For this purpose you can buy lands and houses.

7. Increase your ability to acquire goods.

But when I explain this to people, I find the occasional response is "This doesn't seem anything new or ground breaking, why should I bother?"

And I agree, it's NOT ground breaking at least, not by itself. You see, most people who read the book in which I discovered these principles didn't become wealthy like I did. They still struggle in debt, and watch the world and life pass them by.

Stay tuned,

Dan Cavalli

"Knowledge is power."

Let's forget money talk for a moment. I want to talk about something more important.

You see, there's one thing which frequently crossed my mind when I was struggling and sinking in debt, not so long ago this one thing drove me into action more than anything else.

More than the thought of swimming in cash, or simply stopping those nastily collection agencies hammering down my door...Health.

During my darker days when debt had a tight grip around my neck, I realized that the lack of sleep plus the endless stress and anxiety was causing debt to put a painful grip on my old ticker too.

It's a well-known fact, even mild forms of stress and anxiety can lead to high blood pressure, and we all know what high blood pressure leads to.

I just knew, like you do right now, that I was not prepared to let money problems cut my life short. I had a family to look after. Kids to set an example to. Friends I wanted respect from. It wasn't just about the 52" TV.

It wasn't just about the nice sports car. It wasn't even about the heavy weight lifting off my shoulders as debt finally vanished from my life.

But it's not just the stress and problems of your current situation that cause health problems, it can also affect you on the way up.

As A. J. Reb Materi once said…"So many people spend their health gaining wealth, and then have to spend their wealth to regain their health."

So, that's another thing to look out for. Don't let your efforts to actually live your dream end up killing you off either!

How? First of all, when I show you how to eliminate debt, you'll notice a serious weight lifted off your shoulders. That's the stress saying goodbye.

"Knowledge is power."- Sir Francis Bacon

I just love that quote, don't you? But have you ever stopped to really think about it?

I never realized how true it was until I acquired the right knowledge to climb out of debt and create myself life changing amounts of money.

Sadly, many people won't be so lucky. They'll survive on the common knowledge which has taught them to "just get on with your work" and "accept what you have got".

And sadly, without the knowledge to break free from financial burden or even create wealth in life then they have no choice but to work themselves into old age and resign from life worn down and financially broke.

Sure, that's why pensions are so important but why cut your fun short today in the process? Why not have the best of both worlds instead? After all, you never know what's gonna happen tomorrow.

Without the knowledge to succeed with money and finance, what option is there but to keep paying what the greedy bankers demand whilst struggling to keep up with bills and rising costs of living?

Getting by and saving for a comfortable hospital bed isn't exactly my idea of living life to the max, wouldn't you agree?

I'm not sure about you, but I don't consider it wrong to want a little more out of life than that, do you?

==
"Knowledge is, indeed, that which, next to virtue, truly and essentially raises one man above another."
- Joseph Addison
==

Mr. Addison was right, and still is right. In order for you to elevate your status, gain newfound respect, self-confidence and wealth, and basically get the best out of life whilst you are still young enough to enjoy it then you must acquire knowledge first.

The problem is, there are too many folks out there that insist their "knowledge" is best for you, or will help you. But in reality, many of these misguided, well-wishing folks have no real knowledge in the first place.

They have plenty of THEORY...but sadly, knowledge has nothing to do with theory or wishy washy ideas.

Knowledge cannot exist without application. So I ask you...

==
When it comes to finally escaping debt
and creating true wealth in your life,
who would you rather spend your precious
time with...
==

1. The thinkers and the hopeful

2. Someone who has taken the theory, and APPLIED it in the real world so that it becomes true knowledge...knowledge that he can share with you, and save you many years of frustration, wasted time and wasted money?

If I fell into a time machine this evening and went back 5 years, I could only wish and hope for option 2. But that's just me. So what about you? What path will you take?

Stay tuned,

Dan Cavalli

Bonus... your graduation gifts

Here is your graduation gift! The perfect accompaniment to "The Richest Man in Babylon" is the classic book 'Think and Grow Rich'. You can download it from this link: http://bit.ly/babmod

You've made it. Now that wasn't too painful for you?! It's time to pass on the mantle to someone you know that needs to make some improvements in their financial status.

Just refer them to; http://www.the-richest-man-in-babylon.com I will keep you posted with other resources for your development.

Well done for working all the way through this course. You are well on the way to securing your financial freedom. Continue to use the same determination in moving towards your goals.

That is the end of "The Richest Man in Babylon's Lessons" if you so desire and who want more. Join me in this wonderful world of money and finance on the next section.

Conclusion

Debt-Free living is not a mystery, nor is it reserved for the rich and famous. Debt-free living is possible regardless of income or social status. But you need to make the choice. You need to make the necessary decisions that will put you on the right track.

If you're interested in increasing your income potential, the following might interest you: Get FREE access to my international selling book "Blueprint for Making Millions" at: www.blueprintformakingmillions.com

What to do next

Learn the process of getting out of debt and the making money systems by joining my 16 week coaching Program at: http://www.trmib.com/coaching to find out how to register.

Finish the one-on-one hand-holding 16 week coaching program and get my special gift: Dan Cavalli's famous "Commando Business System" Home Study Coaching Course valued at $2,037.00 for FREE! Take a sneak preview at:
http://www.theultimatebusinesscoaching.]

All the best to you,

Dan Cavalli

www.ingramcontent.com/pod-product-compliance
Lightning Source LLC
Chambersburg PA
CBHW051237170526
45165CB00004B/1470